Book Lures Inc.

P.O. Box 9450
O'Fallon, Mo.
63366

W9-AYA-118

ACTIVITIES
WITH
MYTHS

SECOND EDITION

by

Nancy Karl

illustrated by Jodi Barklage

Printed in U.S.A.

ISBN 0-913839-01-9

Printed by
GATEWAY PRINTING, INC.
4610 Planned Industrial Drive
St. Louis, MO 63120

MYTHOLOGY

Primitive man had three ways of explaining his world: through observation of nature, practical experiences and imagination. Nature was often explained by bestowing everything with life and inventing gods with powers far greater than those of mankind.

Mythology is part science, part religion and part social and moral law. Myths attempt to relate cause and effect, seek to explain the unknown and foster ethics and morality.

The best known of the myths are Greek, Roman and Norse. When the Romans conquered Greece, they adapted the religion of the Greeks to their own practical minds. They gave the gods new names and believed in them with less ardor than did the Greeks.

The Norse gods were not immortal and invincible as were the Greek gods. To Norse gods, a heroic death was a victory and there was always a threat of impending doom.

Each culture manifests itself in its mythology. Comparative reading of myths develops an understanding of individual characteristics and a growing sense of the elements that are universal to the mind of man. Mythology does not belong in the past, but continues to work in our minds today. Science fiction writers of today often borrow from the ancient myths.

Stories from mythology draw upon the imagination of the reader and should be used to nourish the inborn sense of wonder in young readers which is often dulled by the practical aspects of life. Then, too, having had his or her imagination stirred, the student of mythology is encouraged to use mythological content as a basis for his or her own original writing. This is the purpose of Activities with Myths . . to help the student to become a consumer of a unique and lasting form of literature, and to use that literature to become a producer of his or her own unique form of writing.

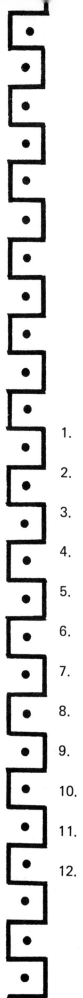

Greek and Roman Mythology pops up everywhere in our modern life! We watch the OLYMPIC GAMES on television. Many cars have MIDAS mufflers. Maps are found in an ATLAS.

Watch advertising on television, in the newspapers and in magazines for one week.

List below as many terms as you can find which come from Mythology. Note next to the term the company or product it is used to promote.

Term   Company or Product

1.

2.

3.

4.

5.

6.

7.

8.

9.

10.

11.

12.

Advertising and Mythology

I. Names and symbols from mythology are frequently used in modern-day advertising.

How many can you name?

a) _____

b) _____

c) _____

d) _____

e) _____

f) _____

g) _____

II. Select (or invent) a unique new product. Write a television commercial to sell your product.   Include in your commercial names and/or symbols from mythology to stress a particular product quality.

1 _____

2 _____

MYTHOLOGY
TIC - TAC - TOE

Complete any three squares across, down or diagonally.
For information consult books on mythology in your
school or public library (Dewey 200s).

all about: _____

What major problem did this god or goddess have to solve?	Change the story (any myth of your choice) by placing the setting in the future.	Describe both the powers and the weaknesses of this character.
Tell how this character's power or powers might be useful in solving problems in today's society.	At what point in his or her life did this person receive unusual power(s)? Tell how they were received.	How would a friend describe this character?
Suppose this character wants to apply for a job. Write a resume stating his or her qualifications for a specific job.	Describe this character from an enemy's point of view.	Summarize the basic plot of one myth by writing it as a cartoon.

TAKE·A·MESSAGE

1

I. One of the following characters from Mythology has called Hermes, the messenger of the gods, to deliver a message. Choose the character who is sending the message.

ZEUS (Jupiter) Chief of the gods

HERA (Juno) Queen of Mount Olympus

ARES (Mars) god of war

ATHENA (Minerva) goddess of wisdom

APOLLO (Apollo) god of light

take·a·message

to:

from: has

sent the following

message:

II. Choose one of the following to be the recipient of the message.

2

APHRODITE (Venus)   goddess of love

ARTEMIS (Diana)   goddess of the moon

POSIEDON (Neptune)   ruler of the seas

HADES (Pluto)   ruler of the region of the dead

EROS (Cupid)   god of love

HEBE   goddess of youth

IRIS   goddess of the rainbow

DIONYSUS (Bacchus)   god of wine

Compose a message which is logical, and is consistent with the two characters involved.

1 Foolishness and greed may prove to be a curse.   Failure to listen carefully will be punished and will cause you embarrassment.

_____

2 Pride will bring about your downfall. Beware of assuming a task beyond your capabilities.   A dangerous journey is in your future.

_____

HOROSCOPES

3 Hospitality to strangers will be rewarded. Be content with your position in life. You and a loved one will share immortality for being faithful.

_____

4 Listen to cautions of a loved one and beware of rash adventures. Flight from captivity will result in destruction.   Grieving relatives will devote life to art and architecture.

_____ and _____

HOROSCOPES

Write horoscopes for four characters from myths.

1	2

3	4

Be sure to include characteristics of
each character in your horoscope.

King Midas

of Phrygia is granted one wish by Bacchus, the god of wine, for doing him a favor. Midas asks that all he touches turn to gold. Overjoyed at first with this power, he soon realizes his mistake and asks to have his power revoked. He was told to bathe in a certain river where his power (and guilt) is washed away. Some say that that is why gold is found in rivers.

If you were promised a favor as was King Midas, what would be your wish? What consequence would result from your wish? Assume that you are royalty.

King/Queen _____ of _____

was granted one wish by _____ for helping him/her

to _____ . King/Queen _____

_____ asked that _____ .

Overjoyed with this power, _____ soon realized his/her

mistake when _____ .

In order to have the power revoked _____ had to _____ .

As a result he/she learned that _____

_____

The Allegory: A Story
to Teach a Lesson

King Midas, cured of his love of riches, now seeks the simple life. He spends his time with the shepherds and nymphs and sometimes with the gods who come to earth for rustic pleasures. On one occasion, Midas is selected to judge a music contest between the god, Apollo, playing on his golden lyre, and the god, Pan, playing on his reed pipe.

Having no ear for music, Midas tactlessly awards the prize to Pan. Angrily, Apollo exclaims, "Midas, you deserve the ears of an ass!" Instantly, Midas's ears grow long and pointed and ridiculous.

Midas is terribly ashamed of his foolish appearance and wears a turban to hide his affliction. However, when his hair grows uncomfortably long, Midas summons a barber and swears him to secrecy. The barber promises to keep Midas's secret.

Finally, unable to remain silent any longer, the barber goes to a nearby field, digs a hole and into it whispers, "King Midas has ass's ears." Then he covers up the hole and goes away.

The following spring, a clump of reeds grows from the hole. With every breeze the reeds whisper, "King Midas has ass's ears."

A. What is the lesson taught by this allegory?

B. Suppose that Apollo had said, "Midas, you deserve the ears of an elephant." How would that change the rest of the story?

C. Create a new speech for Apollo and write a new ending for the story.

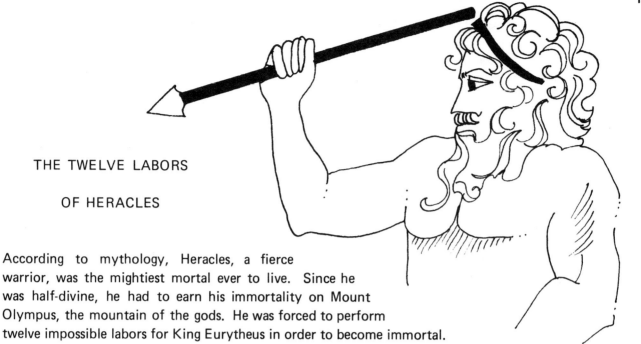

THE TWELVE LABORS

OF HERACLES

According to mythology, Heracles, a fierce
warrior, was the mightiest mortal ever to live. Since he
was half-divine, he had to earn his immortality on Mount
Olympus, the mountain of the gods. He was forced to perform
twelve impossible labors for King Eurytheus in order to become immortal.

You are to accompany Heracles on one of his twelve labors. Choose one of
the tasks listed in the boxes below and plan your strategy to accomplish
the task. Use these six steps to problem solving as a guide.

1. State the facts leading to the problem. Who, what, when, where, why?
2. What precisely is the problem?
3. Brainstorm for as many possible solutions as you can.
4. List what you want an ideal solution to accomplish (your criteria).
5. Examine each of your solutions in light of the criteria you have established. Which best meets the criteria.
6. Choose the best solution and list steps to implement it.

1 Slay the Nemean Lion, a beast no weapons can kill.

2 Slay the Iernean Hydra, a creature with nine heads, one of which is immortal.

3 Bring back alive the Arcadian Stag with antlers of gold and hooves of silver.

4 Destroy the Erymanthian Boar that lives on Mount Erymantis.

5

6 Clean the Augean Stables in one day.

THE TWELVE LABORS OF HERACLES (CONTINUED)

7 Take captive the savage Bull of Crete.

8 Catch the man-eating horses of Diomedes, King of Thrace.

9 Bring back the girdle of Hippolyta, queen of the Amazons.

10 Capture the oxen of the monster, Geryon.

11 Bring back the Golden Apples of the Hesperides.

12 Bring from Hades the three-headed dog, Cerberus

THE TASK I HAVE CHOSEN IS _____

MY STRATEGY:

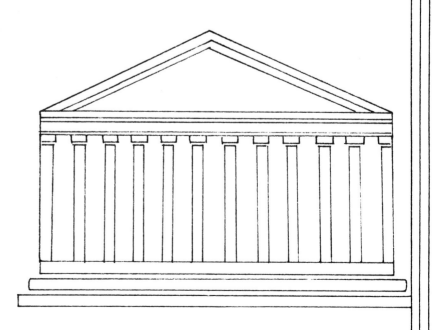

Pyrrha & Deucalion

Because they were faithful, just and honest, Pyrrha and Deucalion survived the flood which Jupiter sent to destroy the earth. They prayed to the gods for help. The oracle answered them, "Leave the temple with faces veiled and garments unbound and cast the bones of your mother behind you." They interpreted this to mean that the earth was their mother and the stones were her bones. Pyrrha cast stones behind her which turned into women. Deucalion cast stones behind him which became man. So a new civilization began.

Pyrrha and Deucalion have asked you to formulate a government for this new civilization. Use your knowledge of history to determine the best form of government for these people and the time period in which they are living . . . past, present or future.

TIME PERIOD

TYPE OF GOVERNMENT (HOW CHOSEN OR ESTABLISHED?)

THREE MAJOR OFFICIALS AND DUTIES OF OFFICE

1. _____   _____
2. _____   _____
3. _____   _____

ONE MAJOR BUREAU AND ITS FUNCTION

WHY HAVE YOU CHOSEN THIS FORM OF GOVERNMENT?

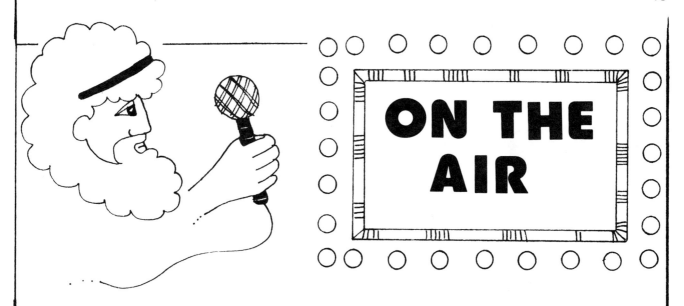

Pyrrha and Deucalion survived the flood that Zeus sent upon the earth to destroy evil mortals. They obeyed instructions from the oracle of Themis and a new race of mortals was born.

You are the interviewer/host on a television talk show. Pyrrha and Deucalion will be your guests. As with all good interviewers you must prepare for the show by reading about your guests and deciding upon the questions you will ask.

A. List the questions you plan to ask Pyrrha and Deucalion.

     1

     2

     3

     4

     5

B. To which of the above questions do you expect to receive the most interesting answer? What will you predict the answer will be and how will viewers react to it?

PARODY

DORANDA

Doranda was the first woman to go to the planet Mars as the bride of the renowned space explorer, Kriston Von Dyke. Among the many wedding gifts they received, she treasured most the gold and silver pentagon shaped box which an anonymous friend gave them. The card said it was a memento of her life on earth symbolizing democracy.

She was disturbed, however, by Kriston's instructions to <u>not</u> open the box, but to be satisfied with enjoying its physical beauty. He felt the box contained something evil, but he had no heart to throw it away. So, Doranda admired and polished her treasured box daily.

Life in the space bubble was lonely when Kriston was not at home. Exploration of the planet Mars kept him busy much of the time and she was not always allowed to accompany him due to the top security work he was doing. When she realized that she was expecting a child, it helped to ease the loneliness and her days were busy with preparations for the first baby on Mars.

One day, feeling especially lonely and curious, Doranda finally decided to open the box. She lifted the lid a little to peek in. But, the force of the contents inside thrust the lid open and out came all the problems of the Earth: inflation, hunger, war, pestilence, energy shortage, corruption, sin, cheating etc. She slammed the lid closed just as the last object was trying to get out. It was trapped inside and has remained there ever since. Doranda closed the lid on some unknown element and preserved it forever. Mars now had the same problems as Earth, but at least there would always be something for the future.

A. What do you believe was left in the box? Predict how life on Mars will be different from that on Earth because this one element which is so prevalent on Earth is not found at all on Mars. Use the back of this sheet for your prediction.

Theseus Slays the Minotaur

The following words are from the Greek myth and describe the scene where Theseus kills the monster.

Choose colorful words to fill in the blanks.

Theseus _____ enters the _____

while Ariadne fearfully _____ outside. From

_____   _____ come the

_____ cries of the Minotaur.   Theseus

follows the _____ through the _____

passages until suddenly he faces the _____

_____ . The Minotaur_____

but Theseus holds his ground _____ .

As the _____ approaches, Theseus _____

his_____ into the monster's _____ .

Then guided by the _____ he finds his way

back to Ariadne.

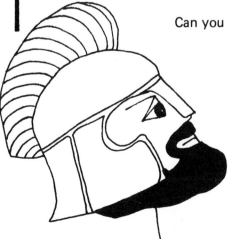

Can you create this scene below?

Invite Your Favorite Character from
Mythology to Dinner!

Dear Mom, _____ is coming

to dinner tonight. Let me tell you
about him/her:

_____
_____
_____
_____
_____
_____

Please serve: _____
_____
_____
_____

Please don't: _____
_____
_____

Thanks Mom. Hope you like my
friend.   Love,

_____

Choose a god or goddess.
Create his or her crest.

Greatest Personal Achievement	Parents' Greatest Achievement
Symbol which best represents me.	My Greatest Wish if I were a Mortal for one day.
My Greatest failure.	Three things I wish to be remembered for.

MY MOTTO TO LIVE BY

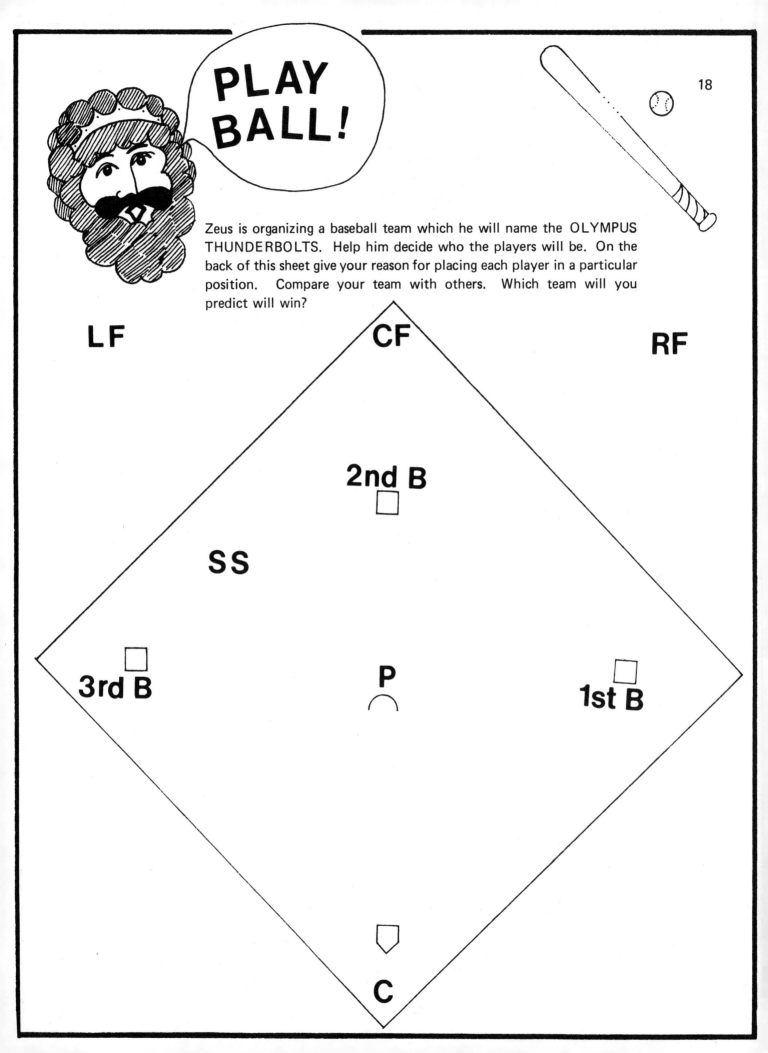

PLAY BALL!

Zeus is organizing a baseball team which he will name the OLYMPUS THUNDERBOLTS. Help him decide who the players will be. On the back of this sheet give your reason for placing each player in a particular position. Compare your team with others. Which team will you predict will win?

18

LF

CF

RF

2nd B

SS

3rd B

P

1st B

C

Mythical Monsters

How sharp is your monster memory?   Match each monster with its description.

1. Medusa _____

2. Minotaur _____

3. Cyclops _____

4. Lernean Hydra _____

5. Cerberus _____

6. Geryon _____

7. Stymphalian Birds _____

a. Serpent with nine heads, one of which is immortal.

b. Giants with one eye

c. Man-eaters with bronze feet and sharp feathers

d. Women with hair of snakes and hideous faces

e. Half human, half bull

f. Three headed dog with serpents tail

g. Three bodies joined at the waist, thus having six hands and feet and three heads

Select one of the monsters described above and elaborate on the description.

ZEUS

Imagine that Zeus is visiting the Earth today. In a group discussion, identify the place that Zeus decides to visit. Identify also, one major problem he finds there.

Example: United States - Energy shortage, inflation.

Discuss several possible causes and solutions to the problem. Write an editorial to Zeus to convince him that he should not destroy the Earth at this time.

PLACE ZEUS VISITS _____

MAJOR PROBLEM _____

_____

POSSIBLE CAUSES _____

_____

_____

POSSIBLE SOLUTIONS _____

_____

_____

You may write your editorial on the back of this sheet.

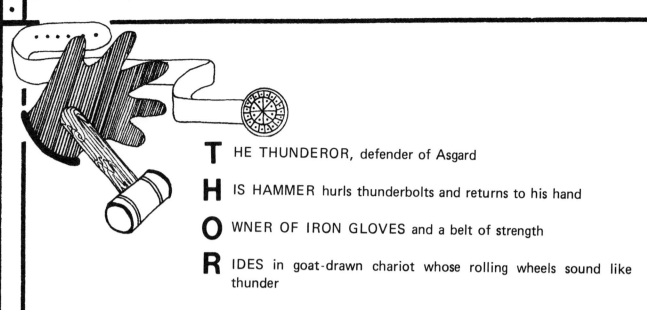

T HE THUNDEROR, defender of Asgard

H IS HAMMER hurls thunderbolts and returns to his hand

O WNER OF IRON GLOVES and a belt of strength

R IDES in goat-drawn chariot whose rolling wheels sound like thunder

Compose a character sketch of the following characters from Norse mythology. Use the letters of the name to begin each sentence.

O _____

D _____

I _____

N _____

L _____

O _____

K _____

I _____

T _____

Y _____

R _____

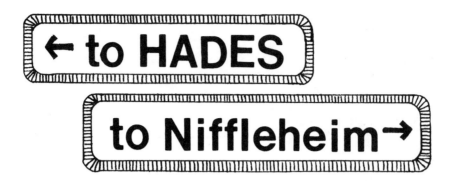

Compare Hades in Greek mythology, ruled by Pluto and Cerberus and Niffleheim, the region of darkness and cold in Norse mythology. How are they alike and how are they different?

Likenesses · Differences

If you had to make a journey to one of these places, which would you choose and why? List your reasons below.

Heimdall

Heimdall, sometimes called the White God, is the watchman of the gods. He sits beside a rainbow bridge, Bifrost, on the borders of heaven to prevent monsters and giants from forcing their way over the bridge into Asgard, home of the gods.

Heimdall requires less sleep than a bird; he sees as well at night as he does by day. He has a keen sense of hearing. He can hear the wool growing on a sheep's back. He carries a horn to warn the gods when Ragnarok, the twilight of the gods, is at hand. Heimdall is Loki's opponent in the last great battle.

You are a messenger from Jotunheim, kingdom of the giants. Your task is to convince Heimdall that you must cross the rainbow bridge and enter the city of Asgard. Plan how you will do this.

WHAT THINGS WILL YOU NEED TO ACCOMPLISH YOUR TASK?

WHAT STEPS WILL YOU TAKE? IN WHAT ORDER?

LIST PROBLEMS YOU MIGHT HAVE AND HOW YOU PLAN TO DEAL WITH EACH

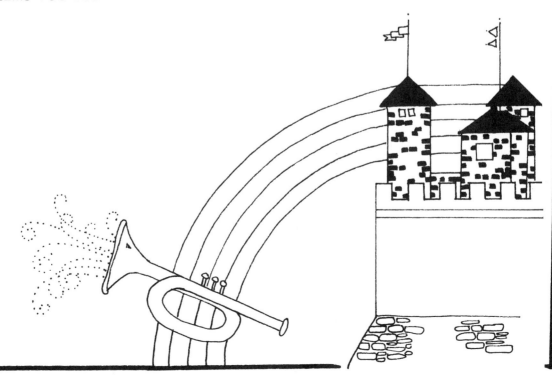

A Eulogy

During the battle of Ragnarok, the twilight of the Gods, Loki and Heimdall meet and fight until both are slain. Assume that Loki, the god of mischief, was your best friend. You have been asked to write a eulogy for him pointing out only his good traits and showing how he tried to make positive contributions to Asgard. What will you say?

MY FRIEND, LOKI

Scandinavian mythology reflects the Norseman's love of battle and conflict. The Norse believed that those who died heroic deaths in battle went to Valhalla, the home of Odin and Frigga. There, each night, they feasted on the flesh of the boar, Shrimner, and drank mead from the she-goat, Heidrum.

The cook at Valhalla has just resigned! You have been selected to replace the cook. Your task is to plan a nutritional menu for one week to feed the brave heroes who are ravenously hungry.

Before planning your menu, you will need to do research to discover what foods were available to the early Norsemen.

You may repeat dishes throughout the week with the exception of the main dish each day.

MENU

SUNDAY

MONDAY

TUESDAY

WEDNESDAY

THURSDAY

FRIDAY

SATURDAY

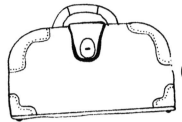

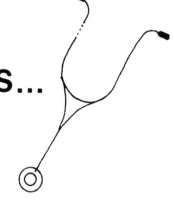

GROUP DECISIONS...

You have just been informed that all the residents of Asgaard, home of the Norse gods, have an incurable disease. You are a physician who has medication enough to cure only one of them. Which would you choose to help and why?

Number the following in the order in which you would choose to save them. All members of your group (if you do this as a group project) must agree on the first and last choices.

_____ BRAGGI god of poetry

_____ ODIN ruler of gods and men, also the god of death

_____ TYR the god of battles who gave victory, law and order

_____ THOR god of Thunder, Odin's eldest son and protector of Asgard

_____ FREY god of rain and sunshine and fruits of the earth

_____ FREYA goddess of music, spring and flowers

R_x prescription R_x

First choice patient to be saved _____

Reasons:

Last choice patient to be saved _____

Reasons:

LOKI AND THE GIANT

Thor and Loki have chosen you to accompany them to Jotunheim, the abode of the giants. You have just entered Jotunheim and are confronted by one very large giant.

Use all five senses to describe the giant.

Looks like: (Use as many words and phrases as possible)

_____

_____

_____

_____

Smells Like:

_____

_____

_____

_____

Sounds Like:

_____

_____

_____

_____

Feels Like:

_____

_____

_____

_____

Remember that Loki is the god of mischief. What trick might Loki play on the giant to get Thor and himself safely past the giant?

(Remember not to always use your first idea. Thinking about the problem a bit often results in better ideas!)

_____

_____

_____

_____

_____

_____

_____

DIAL A DEITY

Suppose that the characters of mythology were living today and you are in charge of installing telephone service on Mount Olympus. Your job is to assign telephone numbers to each of the gods and goddesses using the touch-tone system below.

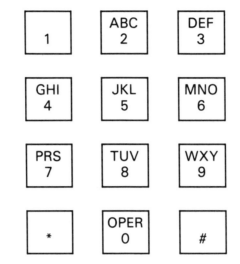

The area code for Mount Olympus is 659. Use a 1 for the letters Z or Q. Example: Zeus' telephone number is 659 – 463 – 1387 (OLY * GOD * ZEUS).

Assign a number to each of the following deities. The GREEK and (Roman) names are listed. The number should reflect the name or some characteristic of each god or goddess. Be creative!

NAME		TELEPHONE NUMBER
ZEUS (Jupiter)	Chief of the gods	_____
HERA (Juno)	Jealous Queen of Mt. Olympus	_____
ARES (Mars)	God of War	_____
ATHENA (Minerva	Goddess of Wisdom	_____
APOLLO (Apollo)	God of Light	_____
APHRODITE (Venus)	Goddess of Love	_____
HERMES (Mercury)	Messenger of the gods	_____

THESEUS—HERCULES

AWARD

Nominations are open for a modern day counterpart of Theseus and Hercules. Choose a real life person who represents the ideal of courage and valor. Design an award for that person. It might be a certificate, a medal, a loving cup or anything else you feel is appropriate.

Carefully letter on the award in twenty-five words or less why the person you select deserves this award.

COMPOSE A MYTH

Compose a new myth involving one of the following characters and a monster of your own creation. In creating your monster remember to give it specific qualities which will play an important part in the story. Your monster can either help or hinder the hero. Choose from the following heroes:

PERSEUS

THESEUS

HERACLES

Consider the following in writing your story:

1. Opening scene (where) and major characters (who?)

2. Incident or two to move the story along.

3. Introduce the major conflict or problem of the story. Who wants what? What will prevent this person from achieving his or her desire. Remember, CONFLICT means opposing forces.

4. More incidents to move the story along . . usually at this point the conflict grows.

5. Introduce characters or events which will help the main character to solve the problem or conflict.

6. Include a climax point . . the point when the hero or heroine meet the problem or conflict "head-on."

7. Solve the problem or conflict.

8. Where is each character at the end of the story?

9. If good triumphs what is its reward?

10. How is evil punished?

11. What lesson about human nature or what explanation of natural events does your story give?

12. Consider performing your story as a reader's theatre presentation with classmates reading the parts of various characters and a narrator reading descriptive portions.

ster!monster?monster!muns